Diamond Vaults
Innovation and Geometry in
Medieval Architecture
Zoë Opačić

Photographs by Sue Barr,
Prokop Paul, Petr Zinke,
Vlado Bohdan

Architectural Association

This publication has been produced to accompany an exhibition held at the Architectural Association School of Architecture in London from 18 November to 9 December 2005. The AA would like to thank the Czech Centre in London and Straropramen for their generous support of the project.

ILLUSTRATIONS
Sue Barr p. 13 and all colour plates; Vlado Bohdan p. 23; National Technical Museum in Prague, Archives of Architecture, archives, file 'Milena Radová-Štiková and Oldřich Rada' pp. 5, 14, 16 (bottom), 18, 24, 27, 28, 33, 34, 39, 40; Prokop Paul pp. 37, 41; Petr Zinke pp. 7, 9, 17 (top), 20-21, 25

Cover: Eisenhardt Castle, Belzig, Gemany, photo Sue Barr

Diamond Vaults was edited by Pamela Johnston and designed by Allon Kaye. Editorial assistant: Clare Barrett.

Printed in England by Dexter Graphics. Paper: Fedrigoni Arcoprint 140 gsm and Symbol Freelife Satin 150 gsm.

ISBN 1 902902 47 5

A catalogue of AA Publications is available from 36 Bedford Square, London WC1B 3ES T + 44 (0)20 7887 4021 F 44 (0)20 7414 0782 publications@aaschool.ac.uk aaschool.ac.uk/publications

CZECH CENTRE
ČESKÉ CENTRUM

STAROPRAMEN

4
Diamond Vaults
Innovation and Geometry in
Medieval Architecture
Zoë Opačić

42
Bibliographical Note

44
Bibliography

47
Colour Plates
Sue Barr

72
Acknowledgements

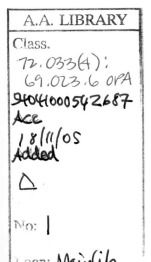

In 1471 Albrecht and Ernest Wettin, then two of the richest men in Germany, embarked on an ambitious project to rebuild their family residence in Meissen, Saxony. The intention was to replace their twelfth- and thirteenth-century castle, which stood alongside the town's cathedral and bishop's palace, with a residence befitting their newly amassed wealth and political status.[1] For the Wettins were not only the lords of Meissen and the greater part of central Germany, they were also prince-electors of the Holy Roman Empire, and second only to the emperor himself in their connections and family fortune.

Over the following 30 years the old fortifications were transformed into a sumptuous palatial complex, which came to be known as Albrechtsburg.[2] The ostentatious exterior of the new Wettin residence – with its decoratively framed windows, shield-bearing gables and extraordinary spire-topped stair-tower – leaves us in no doubt as to the aspirations of the dynasty. Yet even the twisting and angular properties of the spiral stairs do not adequately prepare us for the palace's most flamboyant and innovative internal feature: a series of deeply projecting, prismatic vaults which cover most of the public rooms, stairs and window alcoves. In the Great Hall on the first floor the ribs of the vault spring directly from the freestanding, half-engaged piers spanning the width of the two-aisled interior. The segments of the vault they delineate are not, however, the usual spherical webs, but rather three-dimensional triangular or rhomboidal cells which give the entire surface an origami-like appearance of multiple facets or folds. These unusual creations are the product of the unique imagination of Albrechtsburg's chief architect, Arnold von Westfalen. The overall effect of cut gemstone or crystal has given rise to their aptly evocative name: diamond vaults (also known as cell vaults in German and crystal vaults in Polish).

After their first appearance at Meissen, diamond vaults spread within decades through central Germany to East Prussia, Poland, Bohemia (now the Czech Republic), Upper Hungary (present Slovakia), Austria and as far east as the Baltic states. But their initial popularity was short-lived and after the 1550s they disappeared altogether, only finding a new outlet in the Cubist forms of the early twentieth century. Despite their well-documented origins and their innovativeness, they remain one of the more mysterious of architectural phenomena, little known outside Central Europe.

1 On the history of the old castle and its development see H-J. Mrusek, 'Die Baugeschichte des Burgberges und der Albrechtsburg', in Mrusek (ed.), *Die Albrechtsburg zu Meissen*, pp. 18-30.
2 It was given that name by decree on 15 October 1676, in honour of its founder, Albrecht Wettin.

Right: Great Hall, Albrechtsburg, Meissen, Germany. Faceted forms are a dominant aesthetic feature applied not only to vaults but also to piers, arches and ribs.

This architecture of extraordinary imagination, visual power and technical flexibility, which seemingly emerged from nowhere, is in fact deeply indebted to Late Gothic architectural tradition. Diamond vaults drew on a wellspring of experimentation with geometrical forms, and in particular with novel systems of vaulting which could significantly alter the visual impact of interiors. English and German architecture of the thirteenth and the fourteenth centuries was especially innovative in this respect. The builders of the great English cathedrals gradually abandoned the simple quadripartite vault commonly found in French Gothic buildings in favour of more complex designs. In Lincoln, for example, they added an eccentrically placed rib, in Wells and Gloucester the entire vault was treated as an extension of the decorative window and triforium designs, in Bristol timber structures were evoked in stone. German architects of the following generation, such as Peter Parler, who was responsible for the choir of Prague Cathedral, introduced complex net-and-star patterns into their vaults, thus altering the spatial dynamic of the interior. Stone vaults no longer conformed to the strict bay divisions of earlier architecture but were given their own geometric and decorative autonomy. Their supportive ribs flowed freely in and out of the piers and walls, and converged to form complex geometric or organic shapes.

Despite these innovations, the basic structure of the medieval vault remained relatively simple: the intricate mesh of ribs splayed across the surface of the vault often concealed an almost barrel-like structure underneath. Diamond vaults dispensed with ribs altogether. While there are some earlier fifteenth-century examples of vaults in Germany that incorporate sharply angled planes, Arnold von Westfalen took this principle to an extreme and devised a ceiling of prismatic hollows, where the main aesthetic effect is created not by a decorative interplay of web and rib but by a contrasting play of light and dark across the concave surface.

This stark, 'modern' quality, where spatial geometry is applied to create a unique optical effect, explains the instant appeal of diamond vaults. But there are other aspects that make these structures deserving of a more concentrated study. The creative flourish of Master Arnold and his followers defies the perception that Late Northern European Gothic was a staid and outdated affair, stubbornly trailing behind the latest Classical trends developed by the architects of Renaissance Italy. Diamond vaults

Right: Diamond vaults in the monasteries built by the Observant Franciscans at Kadaň (above) and Bechyně (below) in the Czech Republic.

demonstrate the continuing vitality of Gothic architecture at the close of the fifteenth century, its ability to reinvent itself and adapt to new demands. The vaults are most commonly associated with rich private patrons, mirroring a general shift where secular buildings, rather than great churches, increasingly provided the greatest opportunities for experimentation with new architectural forms. This trend was accelerated by the growing urbanisation and gentrification of many corners of Central Europe, such as southern Bohemia and East Prussia (especially Gdańsk).

While there is no doubt that the rapid spread of diamond vaults was driven by patrons, the creative agency of the architect was also a crucial factor. The fact that the vaults are a datable invention of a known named architect (and his mostly named collaborators) helps to dispel another popular misconception: that medieval architecture was a self-perpetuated, organic process, the work of numerous nameless architects. In his photogenic but idiosyncratic 'snapshot' of vernacular architecture, Bernard Rudofsky placed diamond vaults in the category of 'architecture without architects', alongside Mediterranean houses, troglodytism and pile dwellings.[3] Yet many of the architects of diamond vaults – Arnold von Westfalen, Heinrich Hetzel and Peter Heilmann, among them – were not only known by name, they were also important public figures entrusted with key municipal buildings. The surviving records of several projects (Soběslav, for example) tell us a great deal about the method of construction, including the close collaboration required between the planners, who were often foreign, and the bricklayers, carpenters and plasterers, who were mostly local.[4] Far from being anonymous, diamond vaulting is a flexible technique made distinctive in each case by the combined forces of local tradition and the ability and imagination of the masons who used it.

The flexibility of the diamond vault form is an important dimension. The vaults are geometrically complex but can easily be applied to a variety of interiors and spaces. We find them in churches, chapels, corridors, staircases, palaces and cloisters. Their faceted surfaces also appear as a decorative leitmotif on piers and the embrasures of windows and doors. Arguably, diamond vaults are one of the most distinctive and most versatile tectonic features created by medieval architects. Although not normally found in spaces wider than nine metres – the question of structural stability was clearly important – they fit with equal ease over confined newel

3 B. Rudofsky, *Architecture without Architects*, Albuquerque, 1964.
4 M. and O. Radovi, *Sklípková klenba a prostor*, p. 464, note 50.

Right: Choir of the parish church in Tábor, seat of the Hussite movement in Bohemia (now the Czech Republic).

staircases, cell-like oratories (Kadaň) and soaring aisles (St Mary's, Gdańsk). As we shall see, in several notable examples the vaults were used to renovate interiors which predated them, sometimes by as much as a century (Bechyně). Diamond vaults offered an effective way to give a touch of eye-catching modernity to any structure, and for that reason they appealed to nouveaux-riches and new religious orders, alike.

It is therefore puzzling that this unique architectural feature has received so little attention in English-speaking scholarly circles: to date there has been no single dedicated publication in English on diamond vaults.[5] The present volume is not envisaged as a comprehensive survey, but as an introduction to the subject. It explores the vault's origins, topography, structure and design, as well as function and context, focusing primarily on the Czech Republic, which boasts some of the best examples, and contrasting them with those in Germany and Gdańsk. One of the chief aims is to demonstrate the undoubted aesthetic appeal of this form, which has continued to inspire generations of architects.

ORIGINS

Albrechtsburg's vaults were an original departure in Gothic vault design, triggering a novel trend in Central Europe. However early parallels, if not direct models, exist in Islamic architecture and the structures it inspired in southern Europe, particularly Spain. Islamic architecture frequently used small diamond patterns over a large area, usually as a form of squinch to mask the transition between the roundness of the cupola and the straight wall on which it rests. Segmental (melon-shaped) vaults with sharp ribless edges can be found in both San Salvador de Palaz del Rey in León (tenth century) and Capilla de los Reyes in Valencia (1437-62). In the latter, the material was not brick but carefully carved ashlars bonded into the wall.[6]

Ribless groin or segmental vaults were commonly used in early Gothic architecture (for example, in the choir of the Cistercian church at Heisterbach in the Rhineland). More closely relevant for the genesis of the Meissen style, however, were the vaults with hollowed webs found in the Netherlands, the lower Rhine and Westphalia.[7] In fifteenth-century Saxony the preference was for complex net-and-star vaults, while in the Baltic region of Germany these patterns appear from the fourteenth century and are constructed in brick. But in all these examples, the vault projection is more unified across the surface than in diamond vaults, and the apex is invariably placed in the centre.

The other radical innovation in diamond vaults was the removal of that ubiquitous feature of Gothic vault design – the rib – which affects the appearance of the vault itself as well as the relationship between the vault and the supporting wall. This did not happen instantly. One of the earliest of Master Arnold's creations, the Great Hall at Albrechtsburg, still uses ribs with playful corkscrew bases whose springing points resemble the sharp edges of the vault in St George's in Dinkesbühl (vaulted 1492-99) and the choir of St Lorenz in Nuremberg (c. 1464).[8] The central vaults of St George's were the work of Nikolaus Eseler, whose father, also named Nikolaus, began the construction of the church in 1448. In the vaults of those two architects and their circle, certain ribs are separated from their nearest cells and the latter are given autonomy – a prefiguring of the process of dispensing with ribs.[9] These experiments combined vault summits of flat curvature with diagonal ribs of considerable steepness, resulting in a system of springing points of uneven height, with the diagonal ribs springing from a low point and the transverse ribs from a much higher position. The transverse ribs and their cells effectively 'lift' the vault webs well above the diagonal ribs, leaving large Y-shaped walls between the vault summit, the diagonal rib and the vault cells, which meet each other without ribs at the junction. The system is used early on at a small scale in the Lauingerkapelle in St George's, Nördlingen, by Nikolaus Eseler the Elder in 1447, and later in the Eseler-influenced west wing vaults of Basel Cathedral cloister (by Johann Dozinger, c. 1467). This is also the system used in Albrechtsburg's Great Hall, though with the omission of a number of ribs.

The minutiae of stylistic comparisons provide a means of establishing formative influences on Arnold von Westfalen. The architect came not from Westphalia (as his name might suggest) but from Leipzig, where he was born, c. 1425-30, into a family of town counsellors named Westfal. Not much is known about his earlier training: by 1459, however, he was employed by the Archbishop of Magdeburg as a specialist in bridge construction, and his rise to prominence was assured in 1471, when he was appointed head architect of the Duchy of Saxony.[10] While working for the Wettins on Albrechtsburg and on other locations including Dresden, Belzig and Leipzig, he was also periodically in the employ of the lesser Saxon nobility.[11]

5 See bibliographical note at the end of this book. 6 The vaults were the work of Francisco Baldomar, see M. and O. Radovi, *Kniha o sklípkových klenbách*, pp. 17-21. 7 ibid. 8 Nussbaum and Lepsky, *Das Gotische Gewölbe*, p. 270. 9 ibid. pp. 249-53. 10 E-H. Lemper, 'Arnold von Westfalen. Berufs- und Lebensbild eines deutschen Werkmeisters der Spätgotik', in Mrusek (ed.), *Die Albrechtsburg zu Meissen*, pp. 41-55. 11 Mrusek, *Meissen*, p. 51.

While we do not know what persuaded Duke Albrecht to entrust Master Arnold with the design of the palace, it seems clear that the architect was determined to make his mark from the outset. In artistic terms the residence had to reflect the new strength and ambitions of the family; it was to equal the Gothic splendour of the enormous palaces in cities such as Prague and Marienburg, which incorporated a series of representative rooms intended for official functions of the court. The common designations of the chambers at Albrechtsburg – Great Hall, Great Court Chamber, Dining Hall, Electors' Room and Chambers of Appeal – all evoke specific public roles although, paradoxically, the division of the Wettin estate in 1485 meant that they were probably never put to their intended use. From an architectural point of view, the dignity of the ducal office was conveyed almost entirely by vaults, which transformed what could have been a series of similar-looking spaces into something unexpected. Diamond vaults became inextricably linked with the new aesthetic of the palace, appearing for the first time in underground chambers built into the sloping terrain of the old castle. This area, along with the first floor, is undoubtedly part of Arnold von Westfalen's original design. Also linked to the new aesthetic of the palace are two other signature features: the internal buttress system and curtain arches. The former device – pulling the supportive buttresses inside the structure – was an ingenious way of creating an uninterrupted facade. It also created deep recesses between the buttresses that were converted into generous window niches with characteristic outward radiating arches: the curtain arches. Combined with the cell vaults, these features create an overall effect of constantly shifting tectonic planes: the interior seems to recede before the viewer's eyes, in a series of angular layers.

The *coup-de-théâtre* of Master Arnold's project, however, was the Great Staircase (Wendelstein), which demonstrated the immense creative potential of diamond vaults. Here, the irregular prismatic cells of the vault grow directly out of the stretched triple newel shafts of the winding stair. Its geometric forms masterfully contrast the sweeping swirl of the staircase, and seem to become more crystalline and abstract as they lose their supportive ribs and fan out into a series of arches over the square window frames. In creating Albrechtsburg, Arnold von Westfalen drew on the rich realm of geometric possibilities and on his knowledge of an entire spectrum of Gothic forms, especially those hitherto found in church architecture.[12]

12 See P. Frankl and P. Crossley, *Gothic Architecture*, p. 288.

Right: Great Staircase (Wendelstein), Albrechtsburg, Meissen, Germany.

He also understood that the best way to maximise the visual effect of abstract forms was to juxtapose them to their opposites: the softer features of ribs, balustrades and window frames. The principles set out in the lower parts of the palace were carried through, with only minor variations, by Arnold von Westfalen's successors after his death in 1482.[13]

Master Arnold's designs show some interesting analogies and contrasts with the later work of Benedikt Ried in Prague and Anton Pilgram in Vienna, but there are particularly close correspondences to the double north aisle of Brunswick Cathedral (c. 1469-74),[14] which he must have known at first hand. The ribs of the cathedral aisle wind like cables around the piers and then span the entire structure, creating a continual sense of movement. As at Albrechtsburg, the rounded forms of the piers and ribs 'flow' into the geometric forms of the sharply projecting net vault. The windows, set into rectangular frames with depressed rectangular arches, are also evocative of the flattened window openings in the palace.[15] Though work on Albrechtsburg continued intermittently until 1524, the novel form of vaulting it introduced proved immediately popular. The large number of masons employed, not only from Germany but also from Bohemia, may explain the swiftness of its spread into the neighbouring territories.[16]

In Germany the use of diamond vaults seems to have been exclusively patron-driven, and consequently they appear mostly in secular buildings: castles, town halls, burgher houses and towers. In these spaces we find definitive settings for Albrechtsburg's most beguiling features, for the winding staircase with twisted columns (Wittenberg, Rochlitz), the curtain arches (Torgau), or the vaults erected over a variety of irregular spaces (Annaberg, Belzig). However, very early on a successful Franciscan order led by the energetic preacher, John Capistran, and known as the Observant friars, became associated with the new style and its dissemination. The order founded a monastery in Meissen (pulled down in the nineteenth century) and, with the support of wealthy Saxon-Meissen families, staffed chapels or churches in Leipzig, Freiberg, Annaberg and Dresden.[17] Their progress, aided by close political and family ties between the states, provided a route into Bohemia, where some of the most outstanding examples of diamond vaults are to be found.

13 On the chronology of the works see S. Harksen, 'Zum Bauüberlauf auf der Albrechtsburg', in Mrusek (ed.), *Die Albrechtsburg zu Meissen*, pp. 31-4. 14 The work of Arnold von Westfalen and Benedikt Ried is sharply contrasted in D. Menclová, *České hrady* II, pp. 365-9. 15 Radová-Štiková, *O rozwoju twórczosci architektonicznej Arnolda z Westfalii*. 16 M. and O. Radovi, *Kniha o sklípkových klenbách*, p. 30-1. 17 ibid. p. 38 ff.

Left: Courtyard passage in No. 3, Town Hall Square, Kremnica, Slovakia.

BOHEMIA

At the end of the fifteenth century the kingdom of Bohemia was just emerging from 50 years of religious strife. Once the centre of the Holy Roman Empire, the country had been riven by the Hussite uprising of the 1420s, led by the radical followers of the murdered theologian Jan Hus. It was only with the election in 1471 of a new Polish monarch, Vladyslav Jagełło, that a degree of stability was restored and the court in Prague flourished once more, guided by the creative genius of Benedikt Ried. Perhaps as a consequence of Ried's dominant artistic influence, diamond vaults never appeared at Prague, even though Bohemia and Saxony shared many building traditions, including a fascination with novel forms of vaulting. Nonetheless, in the northwest part of Bohemia links to Saxony remained strong. For the rich burghers and aristocracy, especially, the opulence of the Meissen court set a new artistic benchmark.

The earliest known instance of a diamond vault in Bohemia is in a castle in Doubravská Hora, begun in 1478 for the local nobleman, Jan Ilburk of Vřesovic. The castle's proximity to Saxony and the location of the vaults (in window niches set between internal buttresses) suggests a direct influence from Meissen. Two other early examples of Bohemian diamond vaults are also linked to a powerful man with strong connections to Saxony: Beneš of Weitmil, Lord of Chomutov, Master of the Royal Mint, and staunch supporter of Duke Albrecht's failed bid for the Bohemian crown.[18] It was Beneš who commissioned the diamond vaults in the Teutonic Knights' castle in Chomutov (the present town hall and municipal museum) and Karlstein castle. Although Beneš died in 1496, the work in Chomutov continued until 1520 under the direction of a mason from Eger, Hans Schaffer, who is mentioned in the documents of 1490-91.[19] The vault in the two-bay room on the ground floor of the castle's west wing displays a high level of technical accomplishment, as well as some of the main features of Bohemian diamond vaults. It is based on a four-point star (one in each bay), with a net pattern of smaller pyramidal cells between them. The ridges of each of the star's arms merge at a single point as they join the wall. The springing points are placed fairly low, and together with the vault's deep projections have a monumental effect disproportionate to the relatively modest size of the room (12 × 7.5 metres).

---

18 Albrecht was married to the daughter of Jiři z Poděbrad, King of Bohemia, but failed to obtain Jiři's crown after his death in 1471. 19 The sources are quoted in M. and O. Radovi, *Kniha o sklípkových klenbách*, p. 63 (note 65).

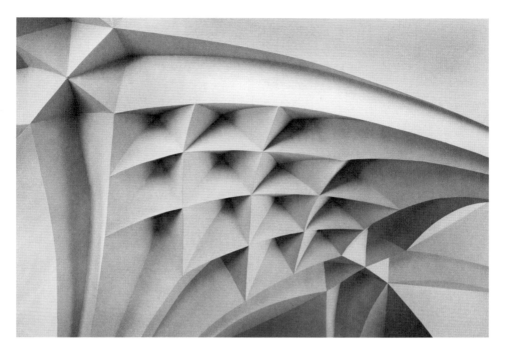

Diamond vaults in Chomutov, Bohemia (now the Czech Republic). Above: Teutonic Knights' castle, now the town hall and municipal museum. Below: Collin-Luther House, vaulted front passage and ground-floor hall.

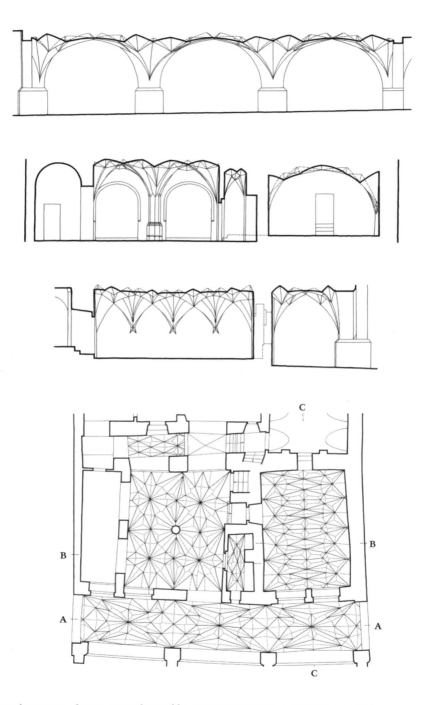

Collin-Luther House, Chomutov, Czech Republic. From top: Section A–A, section B–B, section C–C, ground plan. The architect and the patron responsible for this ambitious project are not documented; however the vault of the longitudinal chamber bears striking similarities with that of the ground-floor room in the bishop's castle at Wurzen, built 1491-97, suggesting a possibility of a direct link between the two workshops.

Although the precise function of this space is not clear, the vaults of the nearby Collin-Luther house (No. 9 in the same square) show how diamond vaults could be used to distinguish important parts of a wealthy household. The vaults, of around 1500, decorate two ground-floor rooms of a two-storey house. The one in the larger room consists of four eight-point stars supported by a single central column. In the adjacent rectangular chamber the low-rising triangular ridges of the vault intersect at the apex, creating a complex net pattern of curving prisms. The intermittent central ridge provides a longitudinal focus, while the two outermost ridges at each springing point join across the surface to form two large hexagons. But it is in the vaulted passage fronting the house that the overlapping geometrical shapes attain their most baffling complexity. Alternating eight- and four-point stars form the crux of this design, with each diagonal rib of the larger star splitting into two to create further diamond-shaped cells close to the springing point. The irregular geometry seems to fold the structure into an infinite number of triangles and rhomboids. The steep rise of the individual vaults contributes to their plasticity and their dramatic effect, which is further enhanced by the changing daylight. The vaults of Chomutov demonstrate not only the inexhaustible fecundity of geometric designs, but also their ability to confer a sense of monumentality on the simplest and narrowest of spaces.

In the nearby town of Kadaň, the newly empowered Observant Franciscans provided a channel for a second strand of Meissen influence. Their first Bohemian monastery, dedicated to the Fourteen Holy Helpers, was founded north of the city walls, on the spot where John Capistran had preached some 20 years earlier.[20] A high quality of workmanship was assured by the patronage of the Lobkovic family, who used the church as their mausoleum. At Kadaň, diamond vaults are found only in the auxiliary spaces on the upper levels of the monastery, which would normally have been inaccessible to the public. The function of these spaces is far from clear. The passage over the north wing of the cloister looks onto the courtyard through three large windows and is separated from the south aisle of the church by a wall. In their admirable survey of diamond vaults, Oldřich and Milada Rada suggest that the passage is an enclosed oratory for the Lobkovic family, comparing it to a similar space in the Franciscan church in Leipzig.[21] But the Leipzig oratory looks into the church interior through

20 On the role and the effectiveness of the Observant friars in Bohemia, see Hlaváček, 'Der Bildungsstreit unter den böhmischen Franziskanern-Observanten am Ende des Mittelalters' in F. Šmahel (ed.), *Geist, Gesellschaft, Kirche im 13-16 Jahrhundert*, pp. 241-7; and 'Lingua contra linguam, nacio contra nacionem' in E. Wetter (ed.), *Die Länder der böhmischen Krone und ihre Nachbarn zur Zeit der Jagiellonenkönige*, pp. 261-7. For the mission of Capistran, see Šmahel, *Spectaculum fidei*, pp. 402-8. **21** M. and O. Radovi, *Kniha o sklípkových klenbách*, p. 66.

three windows, and not away from it onto a courtyard, as it does at Kadaň. Bischoff rejects the idea of an oratory and proposes that the vaulted passage is a later addition erected for some unspecified patronal use.[22] Similar uncertainty shrouds the other two diamond vault interiors. The large, square, double-column room on the second floor of the monastic complex has spacious window seats, and may have been used as a meeting chamber or, as the Radas have suggested, a scriptorium. The cramped two-bay oratory in the south wing of the cloister is thought to have served as a hospital chapel, which would contradict Bischoff's suggestion that the non-appearance of diamond vaults in the main church is connected to the Franciscan pledge of poverty. Kadaň's church, built by the royal architect, Erhard Bauer, and bedecked with lavish funerary monuments, could not be described as austere by any measure.[23]

Further evidence of the compatibility of diamond vaults with the Observant religious aesthetic is to be found in Bechyně, southern Bohemia. In 1490 the newly installed Observant monks began the reconstruction of a fourteenth-century Franciscan monastery, retaining the outer walls of the old church. The presbytery, the first part to be completed, is covered with a simple triradial net vault. By contrast, the taller double-aisle nave uses a diamond vault, with larger and simpler patterns than at Kadaň. The vault rests on three columns placed on the longitudinal axis, and slightly to the right of the choir. Its regular design consists of eight large four-point stars (four in each aisle) which are connected in every direction with smaller cross-shaped cells. The cardinal ridges of the vault curve gracefully into the surface of the outer walls and into the smooth shafts of the columns. The entire design is both monumental and easily legible; the deep hollows of diamond cells and the outstretched arms of the stars seem to echo the expansiveness of the interior.

As at Collin-Luther house in Chomutov, the Bechyně diamond vaults map out the interior of the monastery and are to be found in all its principal areas on the ground floor. The cloister is vaulted throughout by a daisy-chain of large and small quadripartite diamonds that link it visually with the nave. The presence of a pulpit in the cloister may suggest a greater public use of this part of the monastery, which on its east side integrates a chapel, sacristy and chapterhouse, all with their own distinctive variations of the nave vault.

22 F. Bischoff, 'Zur Frage nach der Verbreitung der sächsischen Zellengewölbe', p. 276. 23 The Kadaň tombs and patrons are discussed by Chlíbec, *Náhrobek Jana Hasištejnského z Lobkovic*, pp. 235-44.

Above: Franciscan Monastery and Church of the Assumption of the Virgin, Bechyně, Czech Republic, vault in church.

Previous spread: Franciscan Monastery, Kadaň, Czech Republic. The most impressive diamond vault interior is a six-bay double-column hall on the second floor. The window niches are fitted with seats, and the room is thought to have been the chapterhouse or scriptorium.

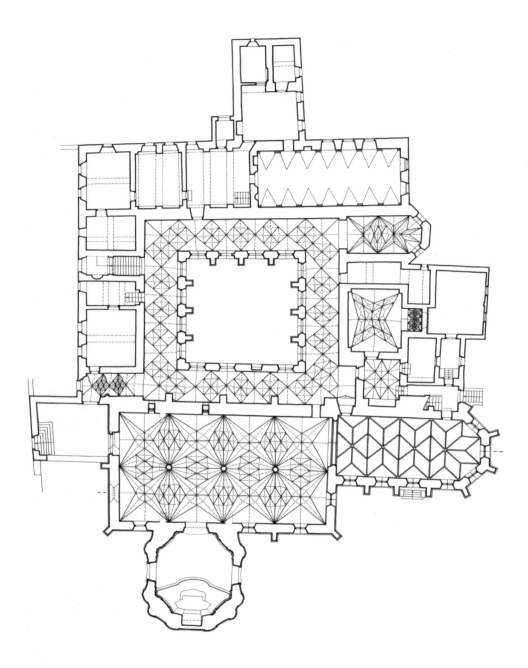

Franciscan Monastery and Church of the Assumption of the Virgin, Bechyně, Czech Republic, ground plan and cloister (right). The cloister is entered through a small diamond-vaulted vestibule on the west side, and leads on the east side to a sacristy, chapterhouse and the chapel of St Barbara, each employing its own variation of the net-and-star design.

Bechyně demonstrated how a new and radically different system of vaulting could be made to serve an existing hall interior – typical of the Luxembourg period of the previous century – and create a unified and well-lit effect. The citizens of nearby Soběslav followed suit almost immediately, employing from 1499 the services of an unnamed master to erect diamond vaults over the nave of their parish church, which had a more traditional rectangular presbytery. The architect in charge must have been the same one who was responsible for the Bechyně vaults, for Soběslav is a virtual replica, albeit shorter, and with a somewhat awkward junction between the vaults and the chancel arch.

The successful marriage of local building tradition and innovative vault design, combined with the support of wealthy aristocratic families, ensured the popularity of diamond vaults in a country not known for its tradition of building in brick. In the Baltic region, however, the transition was more seamless and its outcome therefore less dramatic.

GDAŃSK

Examples of diamond vaults can be found in several regions of present-day Poland. With the exception of the central area of Warsaw, the highest concentration is in the lands bordering eastern Germany and northern Bohemia (such as Silesia and Lesser Poland). The most important examples, however, are in the Hanseatic trading port of Gdańsk (formerly Danzig), on the Baltic Sea, and in the neighbouring territories of the Teutonic Knights. The reasons are once more cultural and political. Strong ties between Saxony and Prussia were reinforced in 1498 by the election of Albrecht Wettin's son Friedrich as the Grand Master of the Teutonic order. Local records of that same year mention a Master Matz, who was probably in charge of the new vaults in the parish church of St John in Marienburg (1468-1523), the seat of the order.[24] In the manner that was to become typical of the Baltic states, the small and shallow cells of the diamond vaults are set only in the clearly separated bays of the side aisles and in the deep window niches.[25]

An even earlier example, possibly the first instance of diamond vaults in the region, arrived directly through Franciscan channels. The narrow diamond-vaulted niches in the Franciscan church in the old suburb (Alte Vorstadt) of Gdańsk are probably from 1496, when the outer walls were

24 M. and O. Radovi, *Kniha o sklípkových klenbách*, p. 309. **25** The vaults were partially reconstructed after 1538, but there is no evidence that they were used throughout the church as suggested by M. Antoni (*Dehio Handbuch der Deutschen Kunstdenkmäler. Die ehemaligen Provinzen West- und Ostpreussen*, p. 394). See also T. Mroczko and M. Arkszyński (eds.), *Architektura Gotycka w Polsce* II, p. 156.

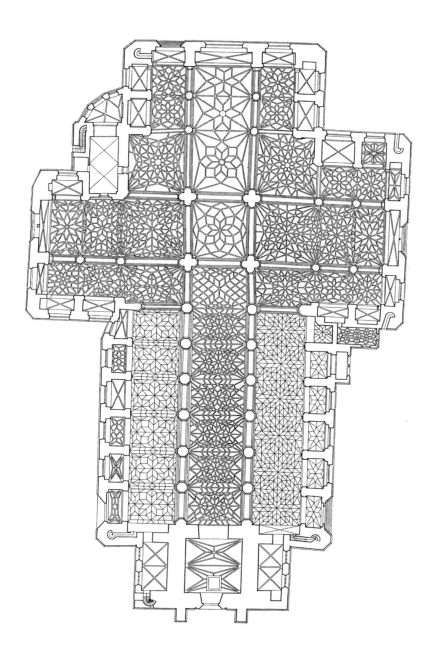

St Mary's Cathedral, Gdańsk, Poland. Between 1484 and 1502, the side aisles were heightened to match those of the choir and transept, and they were furnished with new diamond vaults. The citizens of Gdańsk were encouraged to sponsor the vaults, which were completed at 4 pm on 28 July 1502, when Master Heinrich Hetzel fitted the last brick.

completed. Kaplan dates to this period the rebuilding of the entire monastery, in which diamond vaults occupied several important areas: the north wing of the cloister, the chapterhouse, kitchen and possibly the dining area. The best preserved are the four bays of the cloister, where diamond vaults form regular eight-point stars whose main transverse ridges rest on diminutive consoles. The master responsible for their construction was a priest of the Franciscan order, who arrived with his brothers from 'the German lands'.[26]

The introduction of diamond vaults to Gdańsk coincided with a building boom when several of the principal churches and monasteries were being radically remodelled. The dramatic change of scale in the city's topography is best conveyed by the cathedral of St Mary, whose fourteenth-century basilica was gradually replaced between 1379 and 1501 by the colossal hall church that we see today. The interior of the church combines spatial monumentality with extreme 'economy of form',[27] and its austerity is only countered by the richness of vaulting. Indeed the vaults, rather than the vast open structure beneath them, give the clearest impression of the church's internal structure and liturgical hierarchy. All are domical in shape and they rise, like sails or baldachins, over each bay. The size and position of the individual bays determine the size and shape of the vaults: large net vaults over the crossing and choir, smaller nets over the choir and transept aisles and nave. Diamond vaults are relegated to a secondary position in the nave aisles and the spacious chapels set between internal buttresses, but again the density of the eight-point stars over the south aisle distinguishes it from its northern counterpart. In the ground plan of St Mary's the compulsive rhythm of geometric variations and repetition is strikingly apparent. In reality, however, the effect of the diamond vaults is less distinctive, because of the prodigious height of the nave and the similarity of the eight-point star patterns. At a height of 27 metres, the vaults all but lose their sculptural effect and become gentle ripples across the surface. Placed alongside the plethora of matchstick ribs in the nave, their ribless recesses appear like photographic negatives.

Heinrich Hetzel, who was responsible for the diamond vaults of St Mary's, swiftly became one of the most influential architects in Gdańsk, and his work was copied in churches across the city. In the roughly coeval basilica of St Catherine, diamond vaults are also found only in the side

26 H.C. Kaplan, *The Danzig Churches*, p. 37. 27 ibid. p. 50.

Left: St Mary's Cathedral, Gdańsk, Poland, vault in nave aisle.

aisles. But at 13 metres, they are considerably lower than at St Mary's, and the symbolic effect of folded spheres is accentuated by the use of attached or painted stars, which cover the joints of the vault ridges.

The examples of St Mary's and St Catherine's embody the highly distinctive way in which diamond vaults were used in Prussia. Although they remained more common than in Bohemia, they were never used to the same effect or given the same status as the more popular forms of net-and-star vaults. With the exception of St Bridget's in Gdańsk, where diamond vaults appear over the two choirs, and St George's, Kętrzyn, where we find them also in the nave, they were relegated to side aisles, towers, porches and chapels. Nor did they have the same transforming impact on the interiors that they inhabited. In a region rich in vaulting techniques and familiar with brick, diamond vaults became just one of the many options available to architects, something they could add to their repertoire with minimal structural and technical adjustments.

TECHNIQUES OF CONSTRUCTION

At the end of the seventeenth century Gdańsk's civic architect, Bartel Ranisch, set about recording the city's churches. His detailed surveys, published in 1695, are a precious record of much that was later lost, especially during the Second World War.[28] Ranisch was fascinated by the construction of vaults, and he illustrated his study with measured diagrams of individual vaulted bays and their projections. All but one of his examples are vaults with ribs, but his diagram of a single cell-vaulted bay at St Mary's demonstrates that the method of its construction was virtually identical to that of a rib vault.[29] In each case the architect would begin with the principal diagonal ridge (or in the case of the rib vault, the main diagonal rib) and measure out the distance and the projection of all its subsidiary ridges/ribs in relation to it. Only then would the individual cells be constructed using a free-hand method.

Critical for the construction of all diamond vaults were wooden centrings. After the outer walls and supporting columns (in the case of Soběslav and Bechyně, for example) were completed and the building roofed over, the centring for the main ridges would be erected. A framework of smaller centrings would be constructed around them to shoulder the shorter groins. This was the crucial phase of the construction since the

28 B. Ranisch, *Beschreibung aller Kirchengebäude der Stadt Danzig*, Gdańsk, 1695. 29 Nussbaum and Lepsky, *Das Gotische Gewölbe*, p. 271; Kaplan, *The Danzig Churches*, pp. 87-9; Acland, *The Gothic Vault*, p. 228-38.

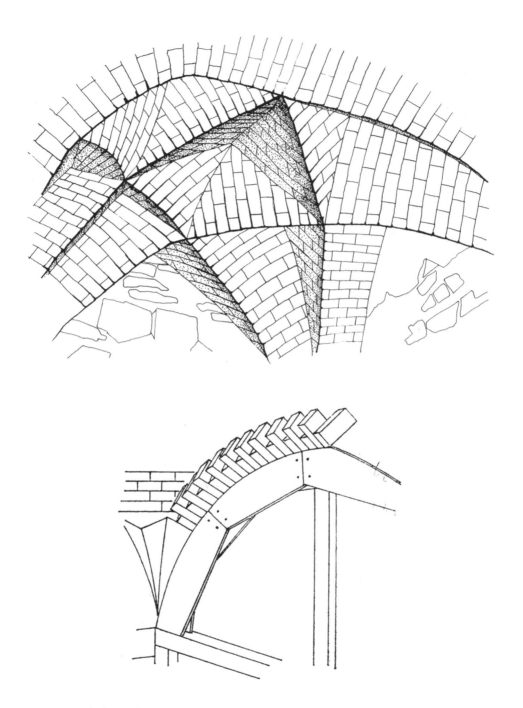

Construction of a diamond vault: diagrams from *Kniha o sklípkových klenbách*. The ribless, curving cells were made stable by the combined forces of thrust, gravity and the mechanical interlocking of bricks.

31

scaffolding for the groins created the layout of the entire vault, and it required a close collaboration between the chief architect and the carpenters. Once the centrings were in place the main ridges would be constructed by laying out the courses of brick with their edges placed upwards and their short and long sides alternating. Simultaneously, three- and four-sided prismatic cells would be constructed across the surface. The angle between the ridges was commonly 45 degrees, since normal bricks could be used without any additional trimming. In the case of wider vaults, another layer of brick would be added as reinforcement, especially over the transverse arches (Bechyně and Tábor).[30] It was common for the principal ridges to be built directly into the wall (either at a single point or 'forked'), although some were supported by stone or brick consoles, or had an elaborate stucco fan-vault base, as at Slavonice. Unlike other, more symmetrical forms of vaulting, the height of springing points could be easily varied across the interior, a useful device in small irregularly shaped spaces such as spiral staircases. In most cases the ridges were constructed at the same time as the outer walls, but there are examples of diamond vaults being attached to an older structure. Sometimes gaps were left in the wall for the transverse arches to be erected later.

The absence of ribs in diamond vaults did not compromise their stability. Arnold von Westfalen's use of ribs in Albrechtsburg's Great Hall may have been born out of concern for the stability of his creation, but it could simply have been a means to distinguish architecturally one of the most important rooms in the palace. However, as ribs obscured the vault's sharp edges and thus contradicted its angular aesthetic, they were gradually abandoned altogether. The ribless, curving cells of diamond vaults were made stable by the combined forces of thrust, gravity and the mechanical interlocking of bricks – a significantly lighter material than stone.[31] Nevertheless, as a rule diamond vaults covered only relatively small spans.

Apart from carpenters, bricklayers and stone masons, the construction of diamond vaults involved plasterers, who had the important task, in the final stages, of creating a smooth, even surface that would cover up any irregularities in the brickwork and enhance the chiaroscuro effect of the cells. Although diamond vaults were usually whitewashed, there is also evidence of painted ornaments: we find floral patterns at Kadaň, for example, while at Gdańsk the joins between ridges are decorated with

30 M. and O. Radovi, *Kniha o sklípkových klenbách*, p. 132. 31 Kaplan, *The Danzig Churches*, pp. 87-9. Acland, *The Gothic Vault*, p. 228.

Right: House at Jindřichův Hradec, Czech Republic.

small discs with painted or attached golden stars. But the most flamboyant decoration appears among the last examples of diamond vaults to be built in Bohemia and Moravia. In the houses in Slavonice, Telč, Jindřichův Hradec and Znojmo, pendant bosses were added to the vault, supported (in Slavonice) by stucco fan-vault bases. The bosses were constructed in a similar way to their fourteenth-century precursors in the sacristy of Prague Cathedral, by suspending a 12-mm iron rod through the vault and securing it at the top with a cross-bar that rests on the extrados of the vault itself. The visible underside of the boss was constructed using bricks and stucco, which were carefully plastered over. These late examples reveal the continuing dependence of diamond vault architects on traditional building techniques. At the same time, builders and their patrons were gradually moving away from these simple but effective geometric shapes towards more elaborate and purely decorative surface patterns. In order to investigate these last examples, we shall return once more to Bohemia.

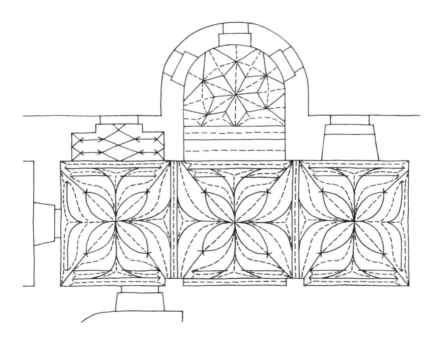

Castle chapel at Breiteneich, Austria.

EPILOGUE: SLAVONICE AND THE TYPOLOGY OF DIAMOND VAULTS

In the 1540s and 1550s a new strand of Czech diamond vault construction, closely connected with Upper Austria, demonstrated a revitalised interest in experimenting with novel features. In the castle chapel at Breiteneich in Austria, for example, we see a new tendency to soften the angular forms of diamond vaults by combining them with petal-like shapes, reminiscent of the designs of Benedikt Ried or Anton Pilgram. At the same time, the vaults of the castle's gallery, resting on round arches and Tuscan columns, combine triradial ribs with pendant bosses – a distant echo of the style of Ried's predecessor in the royal workshop, Peter Parler. These two elements of Breiteneich's design – the four-petalled diamond vault and the pendant boss – were united in the single bay of the town hall of Ivančice, across the Moravian border. This was soon copied in houses in the neighbouring towns of Znojmo, Telč and Jindřichův Hradec, where the boss is suspended from an elaborate eight-point star.

In all these examples the pendant boss is a central element of a single bay only, but in nearby Slavonice it becomes a multiple feature of extraordinary composite designs. Under the direction of a resident mason, Leopold Estreicher, three houses facing the Lower Square (Nos. 25, 45 and 46) were decorated with exquisite diamond vaults in the mid-1540s. No. 25, at the southwest end of the square, is entered through a handsome hall with four eight-point stars, each featuring a ball-shaped pendant boss. The elongated rhomboids of the stars taper outwards into triradial cells whose main ridges spring from the simple consoles decorated with the masons' monograms. Visually the entire vault seems balanced on a single octagonal pier and its square, heavily imposted capital. The cramped space of the staircase hall in No. 45 could not accommodate such an ambitious design. Nevertheless, the sense of rotund plasticity is conveyed here not only by the three pendant bosses but also by their supporting ridges, which fan out from the small cylindrical corbels. In the vaults of the neighbouring house (No. 46), that composition was taken to its natural conclusion: the rectangular entrance hall is spanned by four large fans, uncannily reminiscent of similar English designs, and crowned by two suspended keystones, one partially obscured by a large coffered window arch.

This final flourish of diamond vaults in Slavonice shows them at their most imaginative and eclectic, and with a sense for theatrical decorum not seen since their first appearance at Albrechtsburg. The architect was able to overcome spatial limitations by bringing together Central European Gothic, Italian Renaissance and even English-looking Perpendicular elements, without any apparent contradiction. The result was the most compelling of interior designs, worthy of a self-respecting wealthy burgher.

The Slavonice group confirms the notion that the uniqueness of diamond vaults lay not in their technical innovation or structural order, but rather in their distinctive visual aesthetic and their overwhelming effect on interiors. The transforming power of diamond vaults meant that they were never conceived, or perceived, as an elegant backdrop; they were always a meaningful part of spatial composition. But what exactly did they mean to the people who built them? Why were they chosen for certain spaces – and not others? Was there a hierarchy of vaulting, or a definable diamond vault iconography conveyed through its abstract forms or by its decoration?

On close inspection any strict categorisation of diamond vaults fails: their formal versatility is matched only by their functional plurality. Although originally a secular form, the vaults appear equally effectively and often simultaneously in religious settings. In churches they are frequently relegated to liturgically inferior parts – naves and aisles – in the same way that groin vaults had been in earlier architecture. But there are many important instances where they are found only in the choir and above altars. Clearly in both secular and religious settings the intention often was to highlight places of distinction. In castles and patrician houses these were usually the more accessible public rooms on the ground floor, as for example in the Collin-Luther house in Chomutov, but at the same time we find them in narrow and undistinguished passages and tower staircases. In many examples their existence seems to be related to some particular patronal use, but often that function is ambivalent and opaque. We can also wonder what special distinction had to be accorded to the 'working' parts of monasteries – cloisters, kitchens or scriptoria – where diamond vaults regularly appear.

Attempts to connect diamond vaults with a particular religious order – the Teutonic Knights in the North or the Observant Franciscans in Bohemia – have also proved problematic. The Bohemian Franciscans, supported by their rich Catholic patrons, may have found in diamond vaults an original form that gave their newly founded monasteries a recognisable architectural

No. 46, Lower Square, Slavonice, Czech Republic, one of a group of three exceptional examples of diamond vaults in a domestic setting.

identity. However, there is no evidence that Franciscans wished to make a clean break with architectural tradition, and until Bechyně diamond vaults played only a peripheral role in their first buildings. A close association of any one order with the new vaulting style would not account for their appearance in several Lithuanian Orthodox churches (Malomožejkov and Synkowicze),[32] or in the choir of the parish church in Tábor – the seat of the Hussite movement in Bohemia.

Perhaps more meaning could be gleaned from the original decoration of diamond vaults, which is now largely lost but may have once constituted an important part of the internal iconography. Diamond vaults do not lend themselves readily to figurative and narrative paintings. The rare surviving examples employ mostly painted floral ornaments, highlighted ridges or attached stars – symbolically evocative of an unfolded celestial sphere. In a secular context painted or engraved coats of arms and other heraldic devices identified and commemorated the patron. A different kind of commemoration was provided by a number of uncovered masons' initials and dates, denoting vaults as singular works of design worthy of the artist's signature. But mostly the prismatic cells were left white in order to enhance their optical effect.

In the absence of any substantive decoration, it would appear that aesthetic quality resided principally in the 'pure form' of the vaults themselves. Regardless of their size, complexity or location, the design of the vaults involved an understanding of how the whole interior is shaped through a correlation of its geometry, spatial composition and support system. Diamond vaults had the ability visually to integrate or to compartmentalise interiors; to make them appear to expand through seamless recession or to diminish them by the presence of claustrophobic, low-rising and heavily projecting ridges. They could add an element of playful irregularity to symmetrical spaces, or conversely could harmonise oddly shaped interiors. An important dimension was added by the effect of light, whether natural or artificial, which had the power to enhance their plasticity.

Observed in totality, the development of diamond vaults over the course of 80 years is characterised not by a variation of any particular form or design – whether locally devised or imported – but by a more fundamental interest in spatial geometry, internal dynamics and the vaults' purely

---

32 Kunkel, *Mazowsze i wielkie księstwo litewskie.*

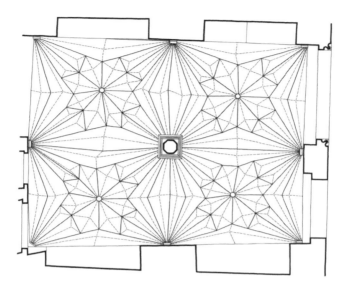

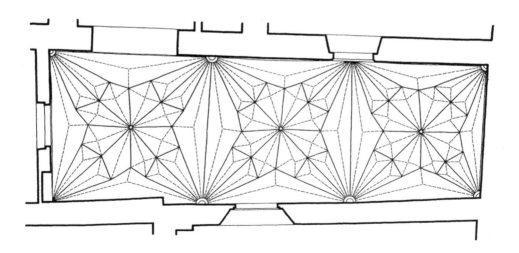

Nos. 25 (above) and 45 (below), Lower Square, Slavonice, Czech Republic. Plans not to scale.

decorative or sculptural effects. Structure and texture – the two defining elements of diamond vault design – are perhaps expressed most eloquently in the late examples produced by workshops in southern Bohemia and Moravia in the middle of the sixteenth century. However, the inspired eclecticism of Slavonice and its circle also marked a creative cul-de-sac for diamond vaults, which were soon to be overwhelmed by the Renaissance forms of the later sixteenth century – only to be revived almost four centuries later in the geometric abstractions of Cubist architecture.

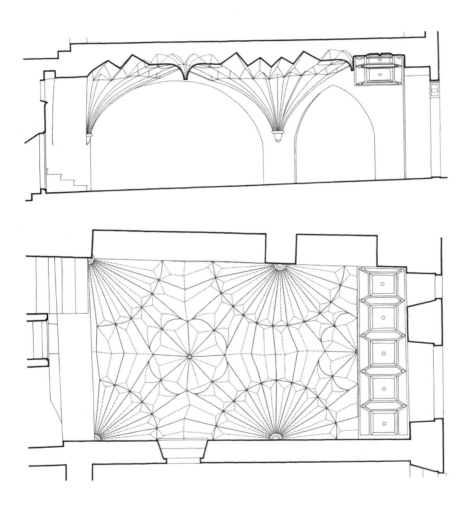

No. 46, Lower Square, Slavonice, Czech Republic.

Top and bottom right: No. 46, Lower Square, Slavonice, Czech Republic. The main doorway and its adjacent window are framed by a single coffered arch, decorated with large painted flowers and foliage. Bottom left: No. 25, Lower Square. The rectangular entrance hall is flanked by two niches on its long sides, and has a small newel staircase at the back leading to the upper rooms. A single octagonal column with a heavily projecting square base and capital supports four bays, each with an eight-point star vault.

BIBLIOGRAPHICAL NOTE

To date the English-reading public has only been able to glean information on diamond vaults from broad scholarly surveys such as Paul Frankl's *Gothic Architecture* or Norbert Nussbaum's translated edition of *German Gothic Church Architecture*. Inevitably for works of such scope, the discussion is confined to a limited number of obvious examples, often leaving the impression that the subject is little more than a passing curiosity. James Acland's study of the Gothic vault admirably dedicates an entire chapter to cell vaults, focusing exclusively on their technical and structural aspects through a series of helpful illustrations.

Unsurprisingly, perhaps, diamond vaults have attracted more sustained attention from German architectural historians. Clasen's standard work on German Late Gothic vaults provides a useful starting point, although it now seems dated. Nussbaum and Lepsky's more recent and geographically broader study of the same subject places diamond vaults in a separate category and treats them not only as a structural novelty but also as a larger European phenomenon, incorporating recent research on examples from Saxony, Poland and Bohemia.

This approach stands in marked contrast to the wealth of regional surveys, where the study of diamond vaults is divided along present national lines. Over the years Albrechtsburg in particular has benefited from a series of articles and monographs, most notably a 1972 compilation of essays edited by H-J. Mrusek which grappled with many contentious issues, from the artistic background of Arnold von Westfalen to the building chronology of the palace. In Poland, the focus was on East Prussia, the region best endowed with diamond vaults, but even here the only available work in English is a 1974 doctoral thesis on the vaults in Gdańsk. Obvious explanations for the presence of diamond vaults in northern Poland can be found in the strong dynastic links between Saxony and Prussia, and the existing tradition of building in brick. In the Czech Republic, however, scholars were locked in a debate over their origins in the western and southern parts of their country. Although the immediate influence of Saxony is now undisputed, the creative independence of the Bohemian workshops, is also acknowledged.

For almost half a century the main Czech authority on the subject was the husband-and-wife team Oldřich and Milada Rada, who dedicated their professional lives to the study of diamond vaults. The crowning achievement of decades of their research came out in Prague in 1998, not long after the death of Oldřich Rada. Published in Czech and German, their book is to date the most comprehensive single study of the vaults, tracing their development from their origins in Islamic architecture to their first appearance in Meissen and subsequent distribution through Central Europe. The book's main accomplishment, however, is the catalogue of all known examples of diamond vaults in Europe, from Saxony to Bielorussia. The absence of a more up-to-date bibliography and the unevenness of some chapters are relatively minor shortcomings in a work of this scale and ambition, and are indicative of the length of time it took to be published. Such minor shortcomings certainly do not detract from the Radas' achievement, which has provided an inspiration for much of the material for this publication and the accompanying AA exhibition.

BIBLIOGRAPHY

J. H. Acland
Medieval Structure: The Gothic Vault,
Toronto and Buffalo, 1972.

K. Benešovská et al
The Architecture of the Gothic (Ten Centuries of Architecture), Prague, 2001.

F. Bischoff
'Zur Frage nach der Verbreitung der sächsischen Zellengewölbe.
Der Nachfolgekreis um Arnold von Westfalen und die Region Nordböhmen', in E. Wetter (ed.), *Die Länder der böhmischen Krone und ihre Nachbarn zur Zeit der Jagiellonenkönige (1471-1526)*, Ostfildern, 2004, pp. 269-83.

M. Brykowska
'Sklepienia krysztalowe:
niektóre problemy', in *Późny Gotyk.
Studia nad sztuka, przełomu średniowiecza i czasów nowych*, Warsaw, 1965, pp. 243-59.

J. Chlíbec
'Náhrobek Jana Hasištejnského z Lobkovic a místo pozdně gotické sepulkrální plastiky ve františkánských klášterních kostelech', *Umění* 44, 1996,
pp. 235-44.

G. Dehio
revised and rewritten by M. Antoni,
*Handbuch der Deutschen Kunstdenkmäler.
Die ehemaligen Provinzen West- und Ostpreussen (Deutschordensland Preussen) mit Bütower und Lanenburger Land*, Berlin, 1993.

K.H. Clasen
Deutsche Gewölbe der Spätgotik,
Berlin, 1958.

P. Crossley
'Peter Parler and England. A Problem Revisited', in *Wallraf-Richartz-Jahrbuch* 44, 2003, pp. 53-82.

G. Fehr
'Architektur der Spätgotik', in K.M. Swoboda (ed.), *Gotik in Böhmen*, Munich, 1969, pp. 322-40.

P. Frankl and P. Crossley
Gothic Architecture, New Haven and London, 2000.

P. Hlaváček
'Der Bildungsstreit unter den böhmischen Franziskanern-Observanten am Ende des Mittelalters', in F. Šmahel (ed.), *Geist, Gesellschaft, Kirche im 13-16 Jahrhundert*, Prague, 1999, pp. 241-7, and 'Lingua contra linguam, nacio contra nacionem. Der Nationalpartikularismus unter den böhmischen Franziskaner-Observanten im ausgehenden Mittelalter', in E. Wetter (ed.), *Die Länder der böhmischen Krone und ihre Nachbarn zur Zeit der Jagiellonenkönige (1471-1526)*, Ostfildern, 2004, pp. 261-7.

J. Hořejší
'Pozdně gotická architektura', in *Dějiny českého výtvarného umění* I/2, pp. 498-534, and 'Hussitentum und Architektur', in *Umění* 40, 1992, pp. 380-4.

H.C. Kaplan
The Danzig Churches: A Study in Late Gothic Vault Development, published doctoral thesis, State University of New York at Binghamton, 1974.

V. Mencl
České středověké klenby, Prague, 1974.

V. Mencl
'Architektura', in J. Homolka et al,
Pozdně gotické umění v Čechách, Prague, 1984,
pp. 74-166.

D. Menclová
České hrady II, Prague, 1972.

T. Mroczko/M. Arkszyński (eds.)
Architektura Gotycka w Polsce,
vols I-III, Warsaw, 1995, especially
T. Chrzanowski and M. Kornecki,
'Pomorze Wschodnie', vol. I, pp.
93-109, and R. Kunkel, 'Mazowsze i wielkie
księstwo litewskie', vol. I, pp. 83-92.

H-J. Mrusek (ed.)
Die Albrechtsburg zu Meissen,
Leipzig, 1972, especially Mrusek,
'Die Baugeschichte des Burgberges und
der Albrechtsburg', pp. 18-30, S. Harksen,
'Zum Bauüberlauf auf der Albrechtsburg',
pp. 31-4, and E-H. Lemper, 'Arnold von
Westfalen. Berufs- und Lebensbild eines
deutschen Werkmeisters der Spätgotik',
pp. 41-55.

H-J. Mrusek
Meissen, Leipzig, 1982.

N. Nussbaum and S. Lepsky
*Das Gotische Gewölbe. Eine Geschichte seiner
Form und Konstruktion*, Darmstadt, 1999.

N. Nussbaum
German Gothic Church Architecture,
New Haven and London, 2000.

M. and O. Rada (Radovi, in Czech) *Kniha o
sklípkových klenbách*, Prague 1998 (also
published in German as *Das Buch von den
Zellengewölben*, Prague, 2001).

M. and O. Radovi
'Sklípková klenba a prostor',
Umění 7, 1960, pp. 437-65.

M. Radová-Štiková
'Orozwoju twórczošci architektonicznej
Arnoldu z Westfalii', in *Podług nieba i
zwyczaju polskiego. Studia z historii
architektury, sztuki i kultury ofiarowane
Adamowi Miłobędzkiemu*, Warsaw, 1988,
pp. 163-72.

B. Ranisch
*Beschreibung aller Kirchengebäude der Stadt
Danzig*, Gdańsk, 1695.

B. Rudofsky
*Architecture without Architects.
A Short Introduction to Non-Pedigreed
Architecture*, Albuquerque, 1964.

F. Šmahel
' "Spectaculum fidei". Českomoravské
misie Jana Kapistrana', *Mezi středověkem a
renesancí*, Prague, 2002, pp. 402-8.

Colour Plates
Sue Barr

I–IV

Franciscan Monastery and Church
of the Assumption of the Virgin,
Bechyně, Czech Republic

V–VII

Parish Church of Ss Peter and Paul,
Soběslav, Czech Republic

VIII–IX

Collin-Luther House, Chomutov,
Czech Republic

X

Teutonic Knights' Castle (now the
Town Hall and Municipal Museum),
Chomutov, Czech Republic

XI–XIV

St Mary's Cathedral, Gdańsk, Poland

XV–XVII

St Catherine's, Gdańsk, Poland

Plate 1

Plate III

Plate IV

Plate VIII

Plate IX

Plate XI

Plate XII

Plate XIII

Plate xiv

Plate xv

Plate XVI

Plate XVII

ACKNOWLEDGEMENTS

This book was produced to coincide with the exhibition on diamond vaults held at the AA in November and December of 2005. Both projects were conceived a couple of years earlier through many stimulating discussions with Irénée Scalbert, whose tactful support and sage advice were essential and enormously appreciated.

Simone Sagi, Vanessa Norwood and Lee Regan ensured the success of the exhibition. Simone in particular dealt with many complicated details with cheerful efficiency and charm. The logistics of pan-European research required good will and support from many quarters. Petra and Jan Eisnerovi made my exploration of Kadaň and Chomutov a thoroughly enjoyable experience. Agnieszka Roznowska-Sadraei, Miki Opačić and Hana Benešovská offered their invaluable assistance. The Czech Cultural Centre was very supportive in many ways. I am also grateful to my colleagues and students at Birkbeck College for their patience with my obsession with diamond vaults. And to my friends at the Courtauld Institute, where I developed my interest in Central European architecture.

In Prague, Josef Pospíšil and his team at the Higher Technical School produced models for the exhibition. Milena Hauserová generously loaned material from her late parents' collection. Pavel Kodera at the National Technical Museum and Dušana Barčová at the Institute for History of Art, provided images from their archives at very short notice. Visual material has been critical to the entire project, and it would be inconceivable without the stunning contribution of the photographers: Sue Barr, Prokop Paul, Vlado Bohdan and Petr Zinke. Sue's photographs formed the basis for the exhibition and her visual essay is an important part of the book.

Allon Kaye's design ensured that images were beautifully organised with the text. The fact that the book exists at all is entirely due to Pamela Johnston, the most patient, incisive and sympathetic of editors. My warmest thanks also to Paul Crossley and Christopher Masters for reading drafts of the text and making many helpful suggestions.

Finally, my deepest gratitude is to Klára Benešovská at the Czech Academy, who worked tirelessly and selflessly in Prague to help us bring diamond vaults to London. All my efforts on this project are wholly dedicated to her.

Zoë Opačić, November 2005